Wool Keeps Me Warm

Mario Lucca

We wear warm clothes when the weather is cold.

We wear socks, sweaters, scarves, and hats.

These clothes are often made from wool.

Where does wool come from?

Children in Russia wear wool clothes to stay warm.

3

Wool comes from sheep.

Sheep grow a thick wool coat.

How does the wool on sheep become the wool that we wear?

A group of sheep is called a flock.

4

A sheep's coat is thick, white and fluffy.

Once a year people cut the wool off the sheep.

This is called shearing.

What happens to the wool next?

Some people can shear over 100 sheep in a day.

6

The wool is packed into bales and put on a truck.
The truck takes the wool to a factory.

Each bale of wool weighs about
330 pounds (150 kilograms).

R. STONE
PYALONG.

9

Combing the wool makes it straight and smooth.

The wool is combed
on large rollers.

A machine spins the wool to make yarn. The yarn is long, thin, and strong.

The yarn is wrapped onto spools.

12

Yarn is dyed many colors.

Now the yarn can be knitted together. A knitting machine can make socks, sweaters, scarves, and hats.

This knitting machine uses many needles to make knitted wool.

14

Now the wool is ready for us to wear!